Other Titles by Patrick Summers

Key Change:
An Alternative History of Mozart

A Collection of Brevities

Birdie's Forever Day

Tapestries:
Connections From an Artistic Life

The Prison of Time: Poems from 2023

The Spirit of This Place:
How Music Illuminates the Human Spirit

52

SUNDAYS

WEEKLY SONNETS FROM 2025
On the Passage of
a Quarter of the 21st Century

Patrick Summers

Contenti Press

This volume is dedicated to the memory of Dr. Margaret Elizabeth Poscher (1958–2025), dear friend and dearer human. Marge made so many lives better than they ever could have been without her.

1

———

To bring the best to all the stuff of life,

One must endure false feelings of success.

The rhymes are not rife: just wife, fife, or knife

And feelings are no more than just a guess.

Strife is the rhyme which we all will ignore

Assuming joy as a type of protest,

Like youthful vows on a faraway shore,

Age is a kindness with which we are blessed.

With promises promised on each new year

Memory softens the wounds of old harms.

We will lose the loves that we hold most dear,

However often we open our arms.

For love, art, and friendship will still abide,

Patiently waiting as all tears are cried.

January 5, 2025

2

Minutes stretch on with the years moving fast.

Words and thoughts eddy themselves in a stream.

What ought to be over has not yet passed.

And what we wish will not be what we seem.

We praise the dear ones who made us better

Those who could answer the biggest big *whys.*

To live truly, we must be their debtor

Striving to take on the role of the wise.

Never before has truth been so lonely

All our worst impulses come to the fore.

What should be ours, we should treasure, only:

Remember that big thoughts opened the door.

The petty will always have a loud voice.

Sing louder, then; there is no other choice.

January 12, 2025

3

I was not ready for life without you.

I understand now I was once in love.

Everything I had to give was in view.

I'm unable to love again, sort of.

For me you have died and so, this is grief.

I carry your heart within me always.

You stole great chunks of my life like a thief.

Which burdens this string of endless Sundays.

Here we are, strangers, as we were before,

Which will finally break my heart one day.

Whatever I gave, the answer was "more."

Could I, just once, have been the word you pray?

    Of all the wonders that can constellate

    The big ones come at the final tollgate.

January 19, 2025

4

The outrage pours forth like a raging stream.

Endless cruelty imposed on the weak.

Everyday urging a new louder scream.

Those who will profit will not be the meek.

For my dearest country, so much belov'd:

Women invented the windshield wiper.

Yet in our faces, small minds are now shoved,

You seem to have voted for this year's viper.

Do you absorb the *real* words that you pledge?

Will we ever learn to live with true care?

Keeping the world on a purposeful edge

Steals the silence in the notes of a prayer.

The spaniel is in his favorite place

Nothing so sweet as the look on his face.

January 26, 2025

5

_____

Recurring feeling of famous faces.

Finding new life in new things I can do.

Help us return to our childhood places.

Stories embracing the *what, why,* and *who.*

Always too soon to farewell a dear friend.

At his grave we listened to "Liebestod."

To live so long yet not be at the end.

As birds overhead set their songs afloat.

Shakespearean edges will never fray.

My best hello was my saddest goodbye.

What am I seeking, and why won't you stay?

My remaining days will each ask me "why?"

 The lengths we will go in finding pleasure,

 Risks missing the true and lasting treasure.

February 2, 2025

6

Comfort in knowing I no longer know.

A thousand lives have passed since we parted.

The price of a new life is letting go.

Of the happiness with which we started.

All ways of living must now be released.

Creation takes everything you can give.

As new things arrive, they must be increased,

Each pair of eyes is a new way to live.

We are all seeking the same moral rock.

Searching becomes its own expectation.

It sits in Browning, and always in Bach.

At last revealing its revelation.

Our life's poem has its own beginning.

Whatever comes, the world will keep spinning.

February 9, 2025

As they strive only to burn it all down,

We serve the needy who need the serving.

Selling their souls in appeasing a clown,

Hoping to cling to what needs conserving.

Can we make art if the world is so changed,

Railing against what they think is elite?

Since all of the norms are now rearranged,

Who will decide who we now will mistreat?

When will we see a return of kindness?

Our souls are hungry for newly found joys.

Flurries of anger ignite new blindness,

And we all become sweet hurt little boys.

Everything now is full anxiety,

As swords hover over society.

February 16, 2025

8

———

Love and turbulence in a place of peace.

Hard to imagine a noble ending.

Every day, chaos seems never to cease.

As art begs us to avoid the bending.

Love cannot be measured by tolerance,

For what if what we tolerate hates us?

Looking within and seeing aberrance,

Will mean that much new horror awaits us.

Suddenly the building seemed too heavy

In its place of honor by the river.

Music and standards are what we levy.

Losing it leaves us alone to shiver.

Please do not let this be my new country,

Since all branches only come from one tree.

February 23, 2025

9

I'm seeing the ruin of my country
Resurgent cruelty on all our streets.
The news runs across our minds so numbly.
Stealing powerless hopes with no receipts.

These times are too sharp and too loud for me.
I was born to love peace and silent air.
We must long to shade our own lovely tree,
Giving back to it what is only fair.

Our ancestors fought and died for this land.
Never complaining or thinking it wrong.
Now traitors sit at their desks, swords in hand,
Ignoring the pleas of the caring throng.

Suddenly, we are a long way from peace,
And the State blusters to us with caprice.

March 2, 2025

10

The best we can do is to make our art,

And bring to the world a dose of beauty.

Too many right now would break ev'ry heart,

So loving becomes a sacred duty.

Above all, you cannot lie to yourselves.

It feels like we summoned the last line out.

Gremlins that harm us convince us they're elves.

The earth longs for rain but it gives us drought.

On many days, it is only Mozart

Who heals the heaviest pains I can feel.

I wake unrested and with a slow heart.

As the softest bells keep struggling to peal.

Happiness breaks through the terrible clouds,

Fending off raiment from being our shrouds.

March 9, 2025

11

Shakespeare is all that is keeping me sane.

Finding the engine of dear old Caesar

Hoping for values I cannot disdain

Working too justly not to displease her.

Loneliness hovers over each new day

Friends check in as I pretend I am fine.

My mind keeps searching itself for a way

For one small thing in my life to be mine.

I know that I can have access to joy:

Whenever I feel my art is needed.

All of my feelings and thoughts will deploy

And happiness settles in, unimpeded.

There is still time to move it all again

Whether it be the baton or the pen.

March 16, 2025

12

Please keep my anger from becoming mean.

I long to put great art into the world.

I have no more need of a Constantine

To keep all the national flags unfurled.

Protect my sorrow from all self-pity.

Use my anger for justice, not vengeance.

Ensure I live in a peaceful city

Kindness is liberty's omnipresence.

Allegiances screaming from all corners,

Creating enemies out of nowhere:

Immigrants, women, and all foreigners,

Are only adults in need of childcare.

Divine energy, help to keep us safe

As all we've created begins to chafe.

March 23, 2025

13

I need a magician to change anger,

Since chaos resides and does not visit.

I want only music to make clangor,

Which is good for the world, I think. Is it?

I'm tired of hoping to find a friend,

Knowing that I am already so blessed.

We get old, yet still we try to pretend

That we're willing to accept one more test.

I wonder if I will still see the world.

Though I know I have walked so many streets.

Old stones have old music waiting, unfurled.

Do not let old hurts repeat their repeats.

    What can we do when choosing joy or pain,

    Except long to love forever again?

March 30, 2025

14

As all of my selves daily have their tea,
Mornings filled with deepest calm listening
Prokofiev Piano Concerti
Vibrate the start of each day, glistening.

Art organizes and unlocks silence.
Geraldine Page in *Trip to Bountiful*—
Or something in the eyes of Mark Rylance
Giving us beauties unaccountable.

Once again life brings me "Send in the Clowns."
What can I offer the world but me?
So much meaning in a small set of sounds.
Has my entire life been in just one key?

I'm living my fullest expectations.
Trying to circumvent all vexations.

April 6, 2025

Summoning angels of inspiration

Brings us close to an earthly paradise.

Music is nothing but suspiration

That leavens the pain of self-sacrifice.

Even the worst storm will run out of rain,

Though many people keep trying to hurt.

A politician in endless campaign

Will always find the right truth to avert.

Of all the things that should/could be wondrous

Why not let freedom be honestly free?

We must not let trouble be thunderous,

Unless we are willing to be at sea.

Why do I feel I was on the last boat?

Look at all we did and the hope we wrote.

April 13, 2025

16

You were the best chapter of my short book.

No one ever spoke my name like you did.

The part of my life I cannot overlook

Was your surprising *pro quo* for my *quid*.

Why do I often feel so newly wronged,

Like a neoclassic composition?

Like a club to which I never belonged,

Where silence is an awful admission?

I am being pulled by an inner force,

In the direction of newer feelings.

Unable to resist their ancient source,

All of my rooms now have lower ceilings.

In all the silence that you left behind

Sadness and joy are always intertwined.

April 20, 2025

_____

The greatest music takes up residence

In the sometimes-territories of God.

Forcing us to abandon opulence

If we do not want to always be odd.

We fight ev'ry day between God and sex.

Each expected to police the other.

But the pleasures continue to perplex

Like some unwanted surrogate mother.

Learning acceptance of what must now be,

How often we have to move on too fast.

But growth is all that is allowed to see

That only what lasts is supposed to last.

Acceptance of oneself is a great gift

To be remembered when one needs a lift.

April 27, 2025

18

There is no one to save you but yourself.

I thought Handel would make a difference,

Wondrous beauties on an endless bookshelf

As the world shrinks, they become a hindrance.

There is no one except yourself to save.

This week was all about *Breaking the Waves*.

Life can sure fuck you, so you must be brave,

A haven for the artistic enclaves.

The building remains but the casts do change,

And we fill the spaces with such feeling,

Only the aspirations rearrange,

Not the wounded feelings, which are reeling.

Spring in Texas is one big bluebonnet.

So, convert the hurts into a sonnet.

May 4, 2025

———————

Isn't it odd that *seven* has *even*

Embedded within its two syllables?

Seven is odd but we must believe in

Words with meaning outside their principles.

Life has a way of always returning

Trying to keep us where we belong.

Realize love's candle is always burning,

Searching for new ways of keeping us strong.

What ever happened to simple dreaming,

Like the dreams we had when we were fifteen?

With everything good, our lives were teaming,

And there was no ugliness in between.

Looking for symbols of other symbols

Has as much meaning as books full of thimbles.

May 11, 2025

To hear the song about Glocca Morra

As played by the much-missed André Previn,

Is to stare into the great aurora

Wherein lies the closest piece of heaven.

Life needn't be perfect to be gorgeous;

You must take the risk, or you lose the chance.

The present moment is right before us.

Who really tells the dancer from the dance?

If you want to go fast, please go alone.

Success is a series of tiny wins.

Remember what is ours; only on loan.

Forget the senseless idea of sins.

      Do it now, before the embers turn cold.

      Later becomes never; regrets grow old.

May 18, 2025

Nothing is liberated by sorrow.

How much of life will you exchange for it?

A show told us it was ours to borrow.

Choose to accept; set all hopes before it.

Their efforts reflect what they think of you.

Who destroys trust without a second thought?

There is no choice but to always love you,

With sorrows and battles so keenly fought.

I have loved him for most of these long years.

Starting over is a chance to rebuild.

Yet even now we are burdened with fears,

Like some wounded, ancient, masculine guild.

    The thoughtful also need to be thought of.

    The cold hand means nothing without a glove.

May 25, 2025

22

Mendacity is a wonderful word,
Though it is far from a wonderful thing.
Whenever you lie, all edges get blurred,
And people who should be singing won't sing.

I know in my life when I've been lied to.
Within my circle of understanding.
In calm retrospect, I would have died too,
Knowing what I know now, notwithstanding.

There is so much we do for our careers.
If you aren't a poet, be the poem.
But even the joys will sometimes be tears.
There will be no better way to know him.

Make this the one thing you could get behind:
If you are in doubt, just fucking be kind.

June 1, 2025

23

What captures this strange unstoppable force?

Does the world need even one more poet?

Desire is an ineffable source.

Each finds a new way to learn to know it.

My life has been flooded with auditions:

My own, each day, and thousands of others.

All of them filled with many ambitions

And in our shared hopes, we become brothers.

Does the world have more beauty than Schubert,

Who seemed to know all about all of us?

His Viennese heart seemed only to hurt.

Affection is the need that is breathless.

The mirror of some elemental tide

Stands before me like an expectant bride.

June 8, 2025

24

For most whom I know, I am far too much,

Spending so much time searching for the lost.

When each day is more longing for your touch,

Would it be better had our paths not crossed?

You have had many bountiful sorrows.

Your smiling eyes make life more beautiful.

May you have a great many tomorrows

And love you're sure is indisputable.

Tristan and Isolde, who find in death

The togetherness that keeps them apart.

Their only common love soon stops their breath.

Mine is the same, when my heart seeks your heart.

When one insists on a weekly sonnet,

The words can only pour truth upon it.

June 15, 2025

All reality will get preempted

In the Michigan earthly paradise.

So out pops the next week's needs, attempted,

As our loving becomes more imprecise.

There is no guilt in setting boundaries

Having been trained to abandon myself.

These are ancient thoughts, forged in foundaries.

There is no more room on my own old shelf.

Sometimes when I'm sad I still look for you,

In each pair of eyes that I encounter.

But it is wishing that I transport to,

As the affection that I need will founder.

This canary was alive before you.

He went in the mine, and I adore you.

June 22, 2025

Trying to figure out what I'm here for.

Heaven might be the color of his eyes.

I'm here defying the things I fear for,

Worried I'll be alone for the sunrise.

Why are we so loyal to distractions?

I fall in love with people who need love.

When joys are parceled only in fractions,

You won't find the one who fits like a glove.

We opened both of our lives like old maps.

The worst pain is loving him in silence.

We love each other despite many gaps,

Which for two deep hearts is pure violence.

There is one thing we always need to grow:

What is a rebel? A man who says "no."

June 29, 2025

I am a lantern, looking for a light.
Whatever happens, I will keep dancing.
Whenever I find him, reason takes flight
But still continues to be entrancing.

Just as blindness comes from masturbation
The zealots will always sell you their lies.
Stupidity is a perturbation.
Surely you can see this with your own eyes.

We leave this life the same as we arrived.
Our last bath will be the same as the first.
Each day it is love through which we revive,
And Mozart will make our hearts want to burst.

Often we think we are seeking closure
When all we want is to hold composure.

July 6, 2025

28

_____

Too many little ones lost in a flood
While politics stays its most indulgent.
It cracks all our hearts and freezes our blood,
While music begs us to be refulgent.

Whatever you do, just keep on dancing.
Why is only the privileged rage heard?
It is not anger that is entrancing.
Our era insists that all will be blurred.

Within the vast mind of Pierre Boulez
Sounds were incised like refractions of light.
I cannot imagine the one who says,
"Melody is music's only birthright."

      The earth refuses to acknowledge us.
      Whatever we do is superfluous.

July 13, 2025

This is a time of cruel harsh losses,

Demonizing the innocent margins.

No one could carry all of these crosses

In expert places, built to be large in.

We are all such grieving and lost children,

Tracing a coldly abandoned shelter.

The fear can only really be killed when

We resign grievances to the smelter.

In this harsh new age of anxiety

Where culture attempts to be protean,

Discerning fame from notoriety

Is the burden that is Sisyphean.

The impossibly gorgeous mountain streams

Stand firmly as symbols of all our dreams.

July 20, 2025

30

_____

Someone I once loved is now a stranger,

Which is a savage new reality.

Could no one warn me of this great danger?

Other than delicate plays by Albee?

I empty myself into open space,

Failing to know the right time for cutoff.

I'm dangling cliffside, in need of a brace

It seems I failed to tell them to fuck off.

Why are we all not tossed from the planet?

A year ago, I did not know today.

The pliable world now feels like granite.

Yet what we carry, we still have to weigh.

I will love again, where I am needed.

Until that day, voices will be heeded.

July 27, 2025

31

A word is the kiss of a stranger's soul.

How I have loved the works of great writers.

All of my life, I have searched for my role,

Trying my best to be an exciter.

I never feel I am fully myself.

I define myself by accomplishment.

The purpose in life is found in itself,

Not in trying to make astonishment.

I am flowing with a long-ago spring,

A story my mind is slowly telling.

It whispers to me about anything,

Creating something that is foretelling.

What will it be? It cannot yet be known.

It sits in my soul, ensconced on a throne.

August 3, 2025

32

―――――――

I have conducted *Così fan tutte*,
One of the gifts of living in music.
It is where love goes when it needs to pray,
And away from Mozart, I get homesick.

Be ever so slow to dismiss yourself.
We think too highly of our own childhood.
The past is an unfeeling devil elf,
Who would have you committed if he could.

Whatever you might have thought you taught him,
That mentee you love more than love itself,
Be sure he knows how to handle autumn
When all remembrances sit on the shelf.

The problems that seem insurmountable
Are disguises of things uncountable.

August 10, 2025

33

I carry what this did not get to be.

I left too much in the palm of your hands.

We both have had too much of the gloomy

To keep on searching for new distant lands.

Maybe it is not about achievement,

Since each moment has a tender purpose,

But fighting this shameful new appeasement

Could reclaim that beautiful word: *anschluss*.

There are moments when I forget his face

Which was at one time inconceivable.

Now I have been gifted with prescient grace

And hindsight makes it quite believable.

In this hugely flawed and dangerous place

Could a healing gentleness find its pace?

August 17, 2025

34

The ancient voices of Aspen valley

Were the resonate roars of dinosaurs.

Now, as we reach this summer's finale

It vibrates with countless acres of scores.

There will soon come a time of elation

When you welcome yourself at your own door.

You have honed much more than your vocation

Once you finally let yourself ashore.

As the trio in *Così* expresses

May all your journeys be peaceful and calm.

The power to ease life's unknown stresses

Rests within music's mysterious balm.

Let yourself be radicalized by joy.

Singing is a life force, and not a toy.

August 24, 2025

What about what we do *not* have time for?

I could not hold both of us and myself.

I feel a force aching within my core

That is both me and not me, and itself.

Can you help to save this beautiful art?

What if all whales went suddenly silent?

There is no *therefore*, described by Descartes.

The message of nature is violent.

No longer let your *self* be a stranger.

An artistic life is the greatest feast.

While the world is a beautiful danger:

Around each corner is an unknown beast.

Write the words that might return innocence

To a world ever more vertiginous.

August 31, 2025

36

The days are filled with all of my music.

It is mine, because I love it so much.

Others might feel this life make one's mind sick,

But music is all that keeps me in touch.

I completely refuse to live in vain.

The music we make expresses our love.

We choose what we love and where to find pain,

So, I write to explore what we're made of.

I hope the last thing we see in this world

Is the great artistic infinity.

In an awareness ocean, we are swirled.

You, me, and us—the perfect trinity.

It's a long time from May to December.

The days grow short when you reach September.

September 7, 2025

_____

Part of my life is becoming a book.

Sentences, with my participation,

Of the many delights which I partook,

In these crazy arts of my fixation.

My dear nation has gone utterly mad.

We are weird, far beyond the looking-glass.

Whatever we thought could be worse is bad,

And we've entrusted the world to an ass.

Once, while we are on the face of this earth,

Could we look at each other in silence?

We never fully recover from birth,

From the traumas that put us in a trance.

We are fishermen in a freezing sea.

With the right love, who knows who we might be?

September 14, 2025

38

Can we now silence our inner judges,
The ones who fight little wars on error?
They only feed on their ancient grudges
And inhibit the gifted torchbearer.

The body grows old, but the child remains,
Exploring a child's native wild tourism.
The wrong care will just put the child in chains,
Drowning in *things*, while starving for wisdom

We have many chances to be bolder.
Why must we promote humiliation?
Joy is the eye of the music holder,
And requires just one alteration.

      It is that moment when our friends get old
      That we must love them again, thousandfold.

September 21, 2025

39

We are all so finite, newly fragile,

While time is old and infinite and strong.

The sole future is in being agile,

For holding to the past will leave you wrong.

We don't all experience the same rain.

Some have umbrellas, and some, leaky roofs.

I have overwhelming joy, but with pain.

That is the agony of seeking truths.

This time has been about *Dead Man Walking,*

The country's old harms that are systemic.

Art is the best way to keep us talking,

And not just screaming the next polemic.

Hold each simultaneous paradox.

Avoid certainty, and question the clocks.

September 28, 2025

Can I ask you to be my Neverland?

A place where neither of us has terror?

That spot in between, where we always stand,

Is not a habitat for an error.

When a musician meets the time of death,

The music remains and we love it more.

What it taught us started and stopped our breath,

A gorgeous Land of Oz behind the door.

Detractors will say you're of big ego,

Never knowing what it takes to perform.

Instead of holding the places that grow,

The art is contracting from cold to warm.

A raindrop is plunging fast toward the earth,

Never once worried about its own worth.

October 5, 2025

_____

When in this world of furious burning,

Do the good you have the power to do.

We have to hold the right kind of yearning,

To keep what is best of us always new.

We are living in a time of monsters

Who have no knowledge of who we might be.

Complicit with them are power's sponsors,

Who only long for us not to be free.

If our minds simply accrue new knowledge,

What are we supposed to do with it all?

We must view our lives as one big college,

And keep on searching for what will enthrall.

People are busy, so give them some grace.

The flowers are reaching out for their vase.

October 12, 2025

42

_____

Someone loves what you dislike about you,

So stop all the second-guessing of him.

None of this nervousness is without _two_,

Since both of us are out on the same limb.

Now that celebrities hate leaf blowers,

Can we at last purge these screaming machines?

Attacking the earth with these flame throwers

Damages nature right down to its genes.

If you are shown cruelty, believe it,

No matter how nice they are afterwards.

You can choose to reject or receive it,

But only by using old Latin words.

      Is it so hard to make a decision,

      Knowing our needs with simple precision?

October 19, 2025

I was not ready for Diane Keaton

To leave the world with movies to be made.

Her smile and laughter would always sweeten

The troubled waters through which we all wade.

It was the same week we lost gorgeous Marge,

Whose name never graced a movie marquee.

Yet she was where I could always recharge,

As her open arms made life more carefree.

Do not take any moment for granted.

We are all subsisting on borrowed time.

Maintain the seeds your love must have planted,

To squander happiness would be a crime.

    I often think I do not have a mind.

    I have feelings and thoughts, not always kind.

October 26, 2025

———

To earn the gift of love from an old dog,

Be prepared for the whole world to feel dead.

For when his short life ends, feelings will fog,

Since with him go the things we left unsaid.

Reading a fine novel by Ethan Hawke,

I remember anew what writing is.

It enters the caverns we often mock,

Those feelings destroyed by the music biz.

The ultimate oxymoron: pure lust.

The physical feeling of loneliness.

All we truly need is a little trust,

And a spot where we can feel coziness.

Our country is being quickly destroyed

While parasite cowards laugh, paranoid.

November 2, 2025

The light of change cannot be embitterment,

Since we give vaporous meaning to things.

Because all we have is bewilderment,

We pretend that fame is the stuff of kings.

On too many days my memories hurt.

Will I be happy or be remembered?

Aspirations continue to assert

The only real things that can be rendered.

The business of art is ugly and mean,

As far from ennobling as it can be.

Still, the art remains something in between,

Striving to be what we hope we might see.

Why do people insist on being cold?

It isn't as though we chose to be old.

November 9, 2025

Dreaming my life has been a *trittico*.

Past, present, future, each in constant war.

Finding colleagues who are *simpatico*

Has been the single thing to most adore.

We overcome our perceptions of past

The things that keep us from enlightenment.

What feels present will always be outclassed

By something disguised as entitlement.

Margie, why did you choose to end it all?

Did you think of how much we all loved you?

You were the one friend who transcended all,

The one of which we only have a few.

      When what has sustained you comes to an end,

      Cling to the duties of being a friend.

November 16, 2025

———————

The picture of innocence and sweetness,
I am missing our little spaniel toy.
I hope he now knows heaven's completeness,
And the truth that he was the world's best boy.

The world is on the edge of violence.
Perhaps this is always reality.
But what we most need are days of silence,
Wanting cello and getting timpani.

We must think of soul as a vast forest
Growing forever through many seasons,
A group of needy voices get chorused,
Each of them with unexpected reasons.

We are alive by just a simple breath,
So why do we think so often of death?

November 23, 2025

48

Uncertainty is not a visitor;
It is one of the bastards of living.
It makes itself a happy resident,
Until you decide what *you'll* be giving.

More than anything, I feel gratitude
Though it might not always come out that way.
Life is rarely much more than attitude;
We all keep too many demons at bay.

Our feelings are the one thing we can turn
To edit ourselves from false conflation.
There are melodies besides the nocturnes
That fulfill the needs of our creations.

Keep your great faith in meliorism,
Lest we allow further despotism.

November 30, 2025

Of what possible use it is to write,

If the moon is no more than a lantern?

We must never give up the constant fight,

Since the great orb's inspiration can turn.

The greatest oxymoron is *pure lust*.

Because nothing invites worse decisions

Than the stupidest sex that steals all trust,

Forcing us to repeat self-collisions.

This strange brief pause between two mysteries,

The bizarre consciousness that confuses,

Can be fine if we accept history's

Contradictory capricious muses.

What is your level of audacity?

Fiends will seek to fill that capacity.

December 7, 2025

50

Do not seize the day; it may get startled.

Ease into the day and treat it gently.

Find the deepest joy and keep it bottled,

And stay in love with it intently.

Do you ever wonder what we're here for?

I remind myself to remind myself.

You can choose kindness, severity, or

Someone else's life you saw on the shelf.

Fanatics and fools are always certain,

While the gentle empaths question themselves.

Let the idiots pull their own curtain,

Trust silence in the gloaming of ourselves.

If you are brave, you are someone's coward.

But please know how much you are empowered.

December 14, 2025

The child I used to be is in me still,

Preening with a child's insider knowledge.

But fear's contagion looks for holes to fill,

Making each day an eternal college.

How much longer will the world keep going?

This question, asked by each generation,

Is really just asking *us*, unknowing,

when we will curb our biggest temptation.

The final killer will always be greed.

It is the one thing we cannot control.

Take what you can, but not more than you need,

For how much remains with your heart and soul?

There is an importance to clarity,

But only as a path to charity.

December 21, 2025

52

It will happen if it is meant to be.

In surveying all of my yesterdays:

You cannot manufacture a ruby.

But what is in front of you can amaze.

The year has crowded itself with beauty.

In the midst of harshness we have made art,

While public servants ignored their duty.

We must make the only choice: to take heart.

Darkness makes us seek illumination.

For brief moments I had a writer's life.

These few sonnets have reached their cessation.

Funny: I thought the only rhyme was *strife*.

    Music is the one word we cannot rhyme,

    Because what it teaches is so sublime.

December 28, 2025

PATRICK SUMMERS

Patrick Summers is Artistic and Music Director of Houston Grand Opera, and a guest conductor of many opera companies and orchestras, a professional pianist, writer, and teacher.

www.ingramcontent.com/pod-product-compliance
Lightning Source LLC
Chambersburg PA
CBHW020608030426
42337CB00013B/1270